FLEMISH

WAVE BOOKS

SEATTLE AND

NEW YORK

FLEMISH

CAROLINE KNOX

Published by Wave Books

www.wavepoetry.com

Wave Books titles are distributed to the trade by
Consortium Book Sales and Distribution
Phone: 800-283-3572 / SAN 631-760X

Library of Congress Cataloging-in-Publication Data
Knox, Caroline.
Flemish / Caroline Knox. — 1st ed.
p. cm.
Poems.
ISBN 978-1-933517-65-0
I. Title.
PS3561.N686F57 2013
811'.54—dc23

Designed and composed by Quemadura
Printed in the United States of America

9 8 7 6 5 4 3 2 1

First edition

Wave Books 033

FLEMISH

HE WAS A CHARTIST

He was a Chartist in his apartment
opening cherrystones for guests at lunch,
cutting his hand and getting lemon in the cut.

Rats! his apartment was on the seventh floor
over the 1920s brick courtyard
with sawtooth dentils and long railings.

He was an allergist when he opened the window
to the blue shadow over half the ceiling.
He was a Zimbalist, a cousin by marriage.

Spraying the hinge with WD-40,
he was a parodist, he was a quietist.
But he was a kabbalist when he opened the book.

When he read the words of Aragon
Les asperges rêvent / sans témoins,
Asparagus plants / dream secretly,

he was a dynast, he was a gymnast
whose T-shirt said IRON-ON.
He was a cubist when he heard Mass

in the Latin rite, which has no epiclesis.
As a humanist, as a panelist,
he put away a glass of workahol.

Yet he was a centrist in a balaclava;
on his plate was baklava:
when in doubt, add food and clothes.

STOVE SEASONING

Four small fires, the first only
kindling sticks, to cool down by
themselves, and the fire dies down.

The second, one log with kindling
and the third two logs ditto,
while fuming oil and paint set off

the fire alarm several times,
and finally a new stove is
seasoned. *Dies irae, dies*

illa, I had to translate in
a ninth-grade Latin project:
On the day of wrath, that day

you shall with flame the earth's race pay,
as David and the Sibyl say. Francis
Ponge, an advocate for things,

an oracle every time, says:
We can't get near our
stoves without turning red.

Stoked with very old
chokecherry, dried and checked,
the new stove has a tiny

low-relief lion on it
holding a hatchet.
It's a Jøtul F 602 CB; the old one

was an Upland 27; we
bought it for $128
in 1979; everyone thought

we were crazy. Well, we offered
this old Upland to the Stove
Museum, who said, Oh no,

we don't take any stove made
after 1935. Fine: with
some help I got the Upland

out to the curb at a quarter
to five on a Friday, with
a sign on it saying FREE

in red electrical tape.
At 6:45 the Upland was gone.
The Jøtul beamed heat

waves at, to, and for us.
I incinerated seven-year-old
paper records in its

"color-range, black to red."
Chokecherry is not the
tree from which they make

Robitussin—that's the sweet
Black Cherry. This is
a weed tree, once a "dispenser

of shade and damp coolness,"
warm enough for here. A canker
burns through chokecherries,

though, and windfalls are full of
huge black ants and other eaters of
xylem and phloem tubes, not

so hot to burn. Tent caterpillars
move into chokecherries and
completely defoliate them.

But to eat the tree's red
fruit burns your mouth; that's
why it's called *choke*, it's so

astringent. Alternately, I sat
staring into the computer
screen at the red Rover

roving on the red planet
and its lander, *Phoenix* by name.
"Nerves and Joy," said NASA.

They cooked soil samples of what
looked like an old red clay
tennis court in poor shape

in Rover's labs. "Bright
Chunks at Lander's Mars
Site Must Have Been Ice,"

NASA went on. On Earth,
as Mariana Gosnell, an
exhaustive ice expert, writes,

"We are still in an ice age,
just a warm period within
it." A red clay tennis court

is slow, and expensive
to maintain: its volatile
red dust flecks off

into the air as paprika
from the Caribbean is
central to Hungarian

cooking. Paprika itself
is expensive, although nothing
compared to saffron. Last

night's supper had been
striper over ratatouille.
We cook on a normal gas

range. Following instructions,
I crushed the rough paprika
with mortar and pestle,

and swirled it with raw
shrimp and so forth,
cognac, lit, in the pan.
The exhaust fan bore savory
esters away into the ether.

K E Y

A maple key, split, and stuck on the bridge of your nose, makes you look funny. Silicon (at. no. 14), a powdered mineral, cleans key and lock by the glitter of tiny quartz facets, and the tumblers open. The lolling medieval allegory *Sloth, like* it or not, is as clueless as we are; the old legend sits on the sofa, in a plaid of moth and *rust, consumes fast-* food. You never know, though: management is usually found in threads fanci *er than labor wears, while the used* book turns out to be a prized and beloved gift. And the proverbial *key is always* —wait for it— coinlike and precious in your hand. It is a tool to make the eye of artifice *bright.* Item: you can knit direct from a photograph, it's like an atlas. Hit me on the head with the telephone! It has a keypad. A maple key, split, and stuck on the bridge of Sloth's nose, makes him look funny. A key gives access to a tone; it exhibits Gibraltar-like behavior.

8

FLEMISH

My sister said,
"All the elements in this painting,
Still Life with Strawberries,
seem to levitate"
(by Isaak Soreau [1604–after
1638],
Flemish, early 1630s
Gift of Mrs. Robert McKay
Cincinnati Art Museum)
DO NOT WRITE BELOW THIS LINE
_____

it said on the postcard of the painting.

"I'll tell you how to levitate
strawberries," said my daughter.
"Hull a quart. Sprinkle them
with half a teaspoon of balsamic
vinegar and a teaspoon of
confectioner's sugar; let them sit."

Still Life with Strawberries, though,
isn't a patch on his *Carnations, Tulips, and Other Flowers in a Glass Vase with*
    Peaches, Grapes, and Plums in a Basket on a Ledge with Cherries, a Butterfly,
    and a Beetle.
Isaak Soreau was a twin, moreover,

and in 1652 his twin, Peter Soreau, painted *Still Life with Apples, Black and White Grapes, and a Walnut in a Porcelain Bowl, Together with Chestnuts, a Pear, Figs, Turnips, and a Melon, All on a Table with a Bunch of Snipes Hanging on a Nail* (*SLABWGWPBTCPFTMATBSHN*). Oh Flanders! A Benelux country, a Low Country.

GIANT CULINARY OTTERS

They were a close family of giant culinary
otters from Suriname. The low growling sound was their
hunger and anticipation of whelk and abalone. Their
even-tempered facial expressions and eyes of intelligence

and stylish whiskers appealed to everybody,
so these otters could have any dish they chose immediately
prepared for them and served by experienced cooks.

I read about giant otters in Jackson Mac Low's poem
anthologized in *From the Other Side of the Century*,
edited by Douglas Messerli. Their low growling was their hunger
and anticipation of shad and shad roe broiled in butter
around the time of asparagus and new potatoes.
You couldn't tell if their growls were from their
mouths or their stomachs, but it didn't matter.

Giant otters have been styled insecure.
It was at Spark in Newport that I first beheld
the giant culinary otters dining, where there's easy access
from the water. Another night,
I saw them, twice as many, sixteen maybe,
at Persimmon in Bristol, similarly maritime;
they had completely taken over the place and were
lying around playing Let's Be Stupid, drunk with nutrition.

WILDWOOD FLOWER

Because pirates had captured the frigate USS *Philadelphia* in 1804,
in Tripoli during the Barbary Wars, Lieutenant
Stephen Decatur and his crew boarded the ship in darkness
to burn it, to keep the pirates from it. And Decatur's faithful

Boatswain's Mate Reuben James, to save his master's life,
threw himself wounded in the way of the pirates;
and so a ship was named for Reuben thereafter, viz.:

because in 1941 Kapitänleutnant Erich Topp,
commander of U-552, blew up the *Reuben James*
DD-245, a post–World War I four-stacker destroyer
(first ship sunk in World War II)
which was escorting eastward Convoy HX-156 past Iceland;

because of all this: in a great rage, Woody Guthrie wrote one of his most
    beautiful songs,
"The Sinking of the Reuben James," asking "What were their names?"
and he set it to a melody he had learned from Pete Seeger,
which was "Wildwood Flower": "The myrtle so bright
with the emerald dew"—a song by A. P. Carter.

Y O U

You should have   seen three   young deer

this   morning come   out of the   green

haze predawn   to eat   away at the

juniper trees   we had planted   between us

and the   highway.   They started   at face level

and chomped down   and then up as   high as they could reach.

Soon there were bare   cedar trunks   with

small green   trees on top.

HARLEY LYRIC

I wanted to PRNDL (automatic writing)
over the geodetics, et cetera, or H
standard with overdrive. I could PRNDL

athwart the isobars or on my BL
Harley MS 2253. People gazed
into the Grand Canyon and said

Oh no, how awful, couldn't
it all have been prevented by
contour plowing and strip farming?

Here comes the education part
—these things are sent to try us.
Ha ha, PARK REVERSE NEUTRAL DRIVE LOW
Ha ha, *Lutel wot hit any man, I syke when I singe, Ase I me rode*
this ender day.

HIS MISTRESS'S RIGHTS

HE DOTH DEFEND

The great dog understood gravitation. She
wished for him. Her dog understood her.
He died. The jays barked. He did not visit Boston.
Her mother thought him a model dog. He
stayed with her, a shaggy ally.
The puzzled look deepened in his forehead.
He was dumb and brave. Talkers embarrassed him.
He sent love. He approved her. He walked behind her.

Her father bought the dog, as large as herself.
The dog knew, but did not tell.
Couldn't the dog walk with her and
Master in the meadows an hour?
When she talked with the dog,
his eyes grew meaning, his
shaggy feet kept a slower pace. The dog was
comfortable, terrifying man and beast,
with renewed activity, was cuffed some,
hurled from the piazza frequently.
The dog was the noblest work of art.

T I O N

paper
bble-puff
leaf Whittier
sior. His
cobbles in
ster grass
rockweed, riparian
excelsior.

ballast for
mediate then
sue paper.

COMPOSITE

Oh hello, Helios! All waves and particles,
particles and waves, *o sole mio*!
Hello, you yellow Lego, heart of gold,
coin of the realm, you exhibit
"strap-shaped rays," says Roger Tory Peterson.

You girasol, you adorable
Jerusalem artichoke
with feet of clay: pig food yes
or (poached and buttered)
people food maybe.

Well, you admirable Della
Robbia, you will tell us what?
That he loves me, he loves me not.
Oh Daisy Mae, oh African daisy,
oh logo for Dell!
Oh Gerbera, baby,
Oh baby food, oh you old *roi soleil*!

SCOTTISH FLEET PATTERN

NUMBER TWENTY-FOUR

A saltwater event, with its airs of tarred line and other fibers:

a storm, a sky of black nonchalance

like a ledge of unmined cairngorms;

in the blue searoads, the nets' pulling.

The boatmen wear their tasks on their backs (I'm upstreaming).

Gladys Thompson the needlewoman recorded the pattern names the guernseys have:

Ladder Stitch, Print O' The Hoof, Anchor, Armada, Triple Sea Wave,

and these words are hers

of Scottish Fleet #24: "I found it on a broad fisherman, knitted

in black wool, and it at once

caught my eye." "The panels go round the guernsey instead

of from the neck downwards," to make the coarse lanolin thing which the yarn forms.

T H E Y

They live in a mobile home
made of Adobe Caslon,
a *boeuf-en-daube* outfit.

(Lorna Sage wrote, "Houses and furniture
give birth to people.") Once they drove
from this abode to the huge

Providence PAC, the Home Show.
A whole house was in it.
"I like the house just fine

and that, but you know
I don't like the location."
It's such a tough

bot project getting
food in the tank,
sneakers on the table,

and gasoline on your feet.
(Mary Wesley wrote,
"Mabs and Tashie had the

same relationship with
their clothes as with their
family, friends, and dogs.")

("'Why not?' asked Mike
Mulligan," wrote
Virginia Lee Burton.)

They saw the decades as
wax stubs of experience
recycled into

incandescent diffusers
for uplighting.
(On moving day, Dickinson

was "out with lanterns,"
looking for herself.)
From the car

radio they heard
Ladysmith Black
Mambazo sing

"Old MacDonald
Had a Farm"
barbershop

in deep sound
intervals which
are trapdoors

in a song or even
mere holes, rests.
They stopped for

caffeine. ("Fire is the
teacher of tea, and
water its friend," wrote

Jason Goodwin.) One
activity was to read
parts of David Jones's

In Parenthesis
out loud, a car game.
(Willa Cather wrote,

"The world broke in two
in 1922 or thereabouts.")
Oh, tired old skullsockets,

ultimate sleepover.
—But the e - i - e - i - o
part sounded like

Palestrina.
This worn runner has
a band of kilim at the end,

numinous and practical
strains you could hear
all over the wapentake:

"May the family be comforted
in the promises of Zion
and Jerusalem," much as

planes land at Stapleton
in the Mile-High City
nearer the tarmac sooner.

ARAGON

The blue coat and the
red snowsuit, the
saucepans with see-through
covers—all go to

the yard sale, the Good
Will, with cranberry
wineglasses too small
and ugly to drink from;

I take off on the highways
I bow and I am gone
I wander in the byways
of Aragon:

> *Par les routes de France*
> *de France et de Navarre*
> *je fais ma révérence*
> *je m'en vais au hasard*

MARSTON

Marston has a new boat.
He carved a handsome piece of teak
and affixed to it
some half-round bronze letters.
What is the boat's name?
What's her name?

Her name is ORTS MAN.
No it's NO TRAMS.
It's SON MART.
My boat's name is SORT NAM.

I bought bronze letters for her.
Her name is TRANSOM,
TRANSOM is her name.

JOAN OF ARC HIGH

These guys go to All Saints
St. Alvin   St. Simon   St. Theodore
with holy cuckoo helium voices
I go to La Pucelle High School
It's fairly francophone
I go to L'Alouette, to Jeanne D'Arc
We honor ALL our students here at Joan of Arc High
Joan said it all: "If you hurt me I will say anything you like
to stop the pain"—Bernard Shaw made her say it
in *Saint Joan*, scene 6—
"but I will take it all back afterwards; so what is the use of it?"

THE EAVES

The eaves drip in dreams and for real too in constant delicate falls of dew
    condensing and recondensing.
The trees drip always at night, dreams or not, hung down with diamonds, and
    both water sounds and animal sounds
recur in the dark, as borrowed and leftover light glances off the textured, mushy,
    or glazed surfaces of nature, manufacture.
The trees overdrip the eaves and onto smaller trees and over large obscure weeds
    reaching up, ombré shadows.
These sounds echo in the root cellar. The least air lifts other weeds
out of sand and silt—jagged serrate species, ikat blades. The weeds are ransacked
by unexpected new rain contributing to the passive dew and riding on a heavy
    wind now
pulling loose and detaching a gutter which, falling, scrapes along the quoins,
    clattering
into the catch-basin; in the drywells, gutter and sash fragments, with runnels
of swill gathering leaves and filth, trellis lath and vines. And the rusted gate,
hinge and hasp buckling backward, shaken off its old posts, is swept away too,
from a dwelling-place destroyed not by fire but deliberately by water,
the abraded house half asphalt shingles and half cedar shakes, luminous cedar
    shakes on the roof
down the deep eaves, asphalt shingles on the ell, in the open yard.

SUBJECTS

You see them through water and glass
(both liquids) and through air
with plenty of liquid in it
—water is moving through the air—
you see the large dolphins animated,
unfractious in their native
drink, going
back and forth interacting with
some sort of rings—in a minute-long YouTube—
in a loop, we see these dolphins again and again
looping through rings, in indirect discourse
ringing through the loops.
We see, you see, dolphins
advertising something
we don't have and
we don't want; advertising
exfoliants and astringents,
humectants,
which dolphins don't
know about and wouldn't
want if they did, the
sloe-eyed ones. They
make us feel free,
silent. "Nature film!
Nature film!" See them

in their independence
through water and glass articulating
dolphin home truths.

"A flashlight, a cam-
era, and a vacuum
cleaner" went into his
left lung by way of
bronchoscopy (video
of looking at wild
horses) on account of
pneumonia, or in-
flammatory disease,
totally conked out:
Levaquin (amox-
icillin) and the
nebulizer (he was
anatomized, and
atomized). So
presently he was
able to read the
summary of mineral
transactions held by
the vehicle distributorship,
whose company logo
a relative had needlepointed.

Three boys on hobbyhorses
they had made themselves
("following the lines of the sap")
out of saplings or suckers
and scrap wood. Three
boys flogging their mounts
with whips they made
themselves out of willow
and twigs. Three
stock characters,
drawn by Thomas Bewick
to admiration,
and then engraved in a
petite oval, in a cartouche
of blank space, engraved
on a sawn end of boxwood,
where the grain is
dense, fine, and hard,
the lines of the sap
like a poem "committed
to the care of a Rock."
It is like a netsuke.
Or in a background:
a basketwork fence,
abraded, but still
the lines of the sap
follow in the warp of vines.

Fifty-fifty good dogs
two of you, old and new oh
fifty-fifty equal good
bleached and grizzled
old dog, long time to
sit and stay, fifty-fifty
new dog new dog new dog
great muscles good as old
equal rights old and new
good dog new dog
old good old good
"Wuffy" and "Chips"
(Why the quotes?)
old pads old feet
fetlock and forelock and
"Wuffy" makes a 90-degree
right turn, his own ear
whacks him across the chops
new pads new feet
fetlock forelock dewlap.

Jarlsberg is Swiss
cheese from Scandi-
navia complete with
holes—but are the
holes Scandina-
vian or Swiss? After
all, "Our lives," wrote

Dickinson, "are Swiss— /
So still—so Cool."
Bleu cheese veins are
definitely greenish. *Black's
Law Dictionary*
is green, and *Gray's
Anatomy* is black.
Brie has no veins.
Once there was a
soft cheese called
Liederkranz, but it
went out of business:
sing a Canticle for
Liederkranz, truly smelly.

Every suite ended with
a gigue; every suite
and every J. S. Bach
Suite for Cello ended
with a proactive gigue;
every play (well, many
early plays) ended
with a jig, as in Hogarth's
inductive and all-
enchanting scene: *The
Country Dance*, a signal
form of curtain call. A
blackish proscenium with

bright and dry colors,
costumes, a circle of dancers,
signals, many old and fat,
some not. The End.
The End The End The End.

SINGING IN YOGHURT

Singing in yoghurt—*chanter en yaourt*—
an ignocent pretends to get you through this:
oh, it's *Pas de lieu Rhône connu*—
it's Paddle your own canoe.
Pas de lieu Rhône connu?
No place known in Rhône? WHAT?

"There was a hypoon, and the ship went underboard."
So I go "*Lorem ipsum dolor sit amet.*"
You need an ignocent.
Yoghurt on the macaroni.
Or macaroni on the yoghurt.

AT MIDNIGHT THE SOUND

of riffling book pages
outdoors. No way:
a large dark bird
thrashing in the birdbath,
must be a thrasher.
One brown thrasher
twice, or two brown
thrashers once. No
moon to speak of and
no wind? Who was
asleep because you
didn't wake me up
when she called but
they didn't call—problems
with number and
attribution. Out came
the moon, with rain,
a moonbow. Until
soon, until beyond
very soon, since later
before about then
before now or after
next time the large dark
bird thrashed gently
but insistently in the

birdbath as if reading
while swimming or was
it two birds, thrashers,
swimming while reading,
or rereading, brown, we thought.

COFFEE CANTATA

A POEM IN ENVY OF CANTATA BMV211 BY J. S. BACH

BARISTA: Please, everyone, be quiet and take note
of lovely Lisa and her ancient dad,
two characters at one another's throat.
She's doing what she can to make him mad.

It's roasting in here! Beanmonger, front and center! Welcome,
everyone, to the launch of the Café Cantata Reading Series, whose
first poet is Enid Moulthrop.

ENID: Poem

Until when they could. For all the court, courtmain; for
heavy, the best.
I was and you were asking everyone why ask
to be Natural Bridge. Is Audrey the dog that ran of rats?
When they did but Marian for all, "Forever and for all,"
with perfoliate boneset arrange-o-matic.
As Roger Tory Peterson wrote, "beezp or peent."
As Roy Lichtenstein wrote, "tsing or bwee."
As Wallace Stevens wrote, "ki tiri ri."

Thank you.

BARISTA: I bring your drinks.
            They look like inks.

            And the next poet is Arnold Blenkinsop.

ARNOLD: Cento Sonnet

            It is a beauteous evening, calm and free,
            And hermits are contented with their cells.
            Cathedrals are not built beside the sea
            To swell the gourd and plump the hazel shells,
            Yellow and black and pale and hectic red
            To one who has been long in city pent.
            Oh, weep for Adonais, he is dead,
                    Whom universal nature did lament.
                            Haply some hoary-headed sage may say,
                            Go, send to me Sir Thomas Erpingham.
                            The curfew tolls the knell of parting day;
                            The house was quiet and the world was calm.
                            Is Decius Brutus and Trebonius there?
                            Earth has not anything to show more fair.

            Thank you.

DAD: Beloved but intractable child,
            your addiction drives me wild!

LISA: Without my cup
            three times a day
            I'll shrivel up,
            I'll waste away.

Sweeter than kisses,
sweeter than wine,
coffee, coffee, you're divine
in the brief trochaic line.

DAD: Lisa, no date,
no bars, no mate,
no jocks, no guys:
Lisa, no gown, no wedding feast.
To socialize,
decaffeinate.

LISA: Father, you disgusting beast!
But I'll accede in this at least.

BARISTA: It's explicated by the Bard for you
in *As You Like It*, in scene 3, act 2.

And now—the Mops

MOPS: We are the Mops
From Mopsuestia
We think we're tops
We read *Izvestia*
Here come the cops
They hate our guts
They think we're fops
We think they're sluts
We're full of fustian
We're so Procrustean, etc. etc. etc.

LISA: [*Aside*] Seeking suitable beaux
gladly my father goes
and little my heart he knows:

it shall be sworn in the prenup
I'll brew a pot and drink it up
whenever I desire a cup.

DAD: I'm off to town a husband to produce.

BARISTA: I'd like to think that I could be of use.

LISA: Your offer I accept.
I'll marry an adept.
Dearest heart,
we'll never part.

Come to our *fête*!
We're *faux* Old French
We're *Aucassin et Nicolete*
and he's my mensch.

I'm his star—
He's my buck—
I'm his inamorata—
Here endeth the cantata.

WHERE

Would you like to ride on that boat (a wobbly one)?
They have boats called punts at Oxford for frog-parties.
What they really are is Pogo boats, and they're pretty
but without any of the dignified speed which accompanies a sharp prow.

People are now applying to colleges—DePauw, Fordham, Ohio Wesleyan.
Getting in on geographical distribution is fortunately lying fallow.
Ourselves enjoyed a small outfit to the east
where we "imaged forth" other applying elsewhere.

Rustic solutions abound, but so do cavalier judgments.
The Homestead Act should not be confused with the Volstead Act.
Using the language (exclusively) of an arcane discipline to describe life as tolerable
bores everyone, at all times, and eventually reveals a latent maudlin.

Sensible people close with astringent concern
deeply immured in which is a kind of daring
exemplified by women who put raspberries in their hats
(as it were migrants, which they are) not bothering what people will think.

IF YOU ARE NEARSIGHTED

and sorrowful,
if your eyes are full of tears,

put the open book on the floor,
stand up straight, look down.

Your tears are contact lenses.
You read the book.

What do you think you are
doing? You look feeble!

KEVIN

Kevin, it wasn't a man, it was me,
or maybe it was my aunt, who wore a green suede skirt;
whoever it was, you didn't get a breadfruit—
it was goulash, all paprika and fire.
The donor didn't know when you'd eat;
you were completely grateful and reliable
in the wand of the learning annex.
But your name wasn't Kevin, it was Dirk,
and as you left you said,
"When Calvin was born, Chaucer had only been dead for 109 years."

THE FONT IS FULL OF FISH

at our parish,
fish with sleek fins
and moving between worlds,

while the font on this
fin, this Abe fiver,
appears three-dimensional,

subscribed in the fist of
Anna Escobedo Cabral,
Treasurer of the United States.

Our font is full of construction-
paper fish, made by
the church school for us to

each take home one of,
a reverse tithe. No
water, just colored

paper fish in our font,
which is made of *vrai*
Carrara marble, a

solid one, solid as
the font of Abe's
3-D lettering.

I put mine on the dash
of my car. No fins
on this vehicle.

My fish started out
navy blue, of course,
but now it's white, a

paper-white fish, a sun-
bleached whitefish,
genus *Coregonus*.

Anyway: Carrara.
"Get out your
Carrara notes," said one

distinguished artisan
to another in my
hearing. This involved

going to the beach for gull
feathers, which happen
to be marble-colored. And

to Benjamin Moore for a
gallon of Decorator White
alkyd enamel and a quart

of black; all to make
a faux marble fireplace
out of a fireproof

Sheetrock one. Over the
gull color, feathers dipped
in various dark grays

mimic the veins and
matrix of Carrara,
as the random streaks

drag crosswise along
the whole zone. When
dry, the surface received

two coats of poly-
urethane. Anyway:
a font, a typeface,

a fist, a fin: what
you're reading is
Trump Medieval

backed by a fistful
of Abe fivers and of
Benjamins (Franklin, not

Moore) backed in turn
by specie in the
United States Treasury.

THE SCOTTISH PLAY

The Scottish play the bagpipes with dignity to escort people from here to there. You can read about this in *Wee Gillis*. An English teacher was teaching himself Finnish: "Every morning my wife and daughters ask me, Have you finished your Finnish?" Well, had he? Finnan Haddie! It's an appealing idea, costumed musicians accompanying you wherever you go. Bath is an antithesis of Scotland, fount vs. tarn. Elsewhere, a mighty pinto was named Atlas not because he was strong (which he was) but because his markings described the Americas. Suppose you are headed up the crags to visit this tarn. In the US your car has bumpers; in the UK, guards. *Bumpers* is defeatist, isn't it? As if you *knew* you'd crash. This text could be set in Helvetica.

HE LIVES IN BAYONNE

The band a blonde prefers is called
Bonsai Yggdrasil and it's based

in Wichita. He lives in Bayonne
who grates the nutmeg with a rasp

in his throat. We consume Fabulon.
They sing in Finnish at the Old Folks' Home

Byron's "She Walks in Beauty like the Night."
It snows in Tampa as a ghoulish trope.

He was taken by the passive voice
whenas he committed add/drop with his peers.
You gave an actuary a wall pocket.

He e-mails her a blank screen. She e-mails him
her Trash icon by attachment; nevertheless,
they live in San José with their infant son.

SOCIETY

You could be a politician, you could be a scientist,
    you could be a political scientist, or drive a train;
you could be a Christian, you could be a writer,
    you could write Christian Science fiction.
You could, and it would be asking too much, you
    could believe in salvation
by faith alone. You could be civil.
    You could be in the Peace
Corps, in Arnie's Army, you could be in the
    Salvation Army Corps of Civil Engineers.

We could be in publishing and part of the landscape; we could be a boxer,
    we could be a prophet or an actor:
we could be Muhammad Ali MacGraw-Hill. We could be in the
    Society of Jesus, we could be from Cincinnati,
city of the Society of the Cincinnati, from which my brother
    resigned, *twice*, and city of WKRP,
and of Frances Trollope and Harriet Beecher Stowe;
    city of my mother's ball team, the
Cincinnati Phillies, for whom Jesús Alou did not play,
    and birthplace of Kenneth Koch.

YEAR AFTER YEAR

The mower releases a scent
of autumnal flat creeping thyme.
Not only thyme but salt, magical seasonings.
Among those present,
the fox's bark, the sound of owl's wings.

Hence this set piece in ode mode with end rhyme,
but not standing on ceremony
beside flora that hurricanes volunteer
and granite outcroppings, a natural history,
hand over hand and year after year.

I'M GOING TO RUPERT'S LAND

which you have barely heard of.
We may be experiencing
the Euripides Shift: he made the chorus
half the show instead of just a tenth.
So is it with the Internet.

I've barely heard of Rupert's Land myself;
you may know it takes the shape it needs.
And you have spent twelve years online. Live forever!
Later from me. Best of British luck! We accept the omen. They sloped off.

NOTES

"Stove Seasoning": Line 66, "Phoenix Mars Landing: Nerves and Joy," video, nasa.gov news archives (May 25, 2008); Lines 71–72, "Bright Chunks at Phoenix Lander's Mars Site Must Have Been Ice," Phoenix Mars Mission website, phoenix.lpl.arizona.edu (June 19, 2008); Lines 80–82: Mariana Gosnell, *Ice* (New York, 2005), 6.

"Harley Lyric": The last two lines quote first lines of Harley Lyrics in BL Harley MS 2253.

"His Mistress's Rights He Doth Defend": The poem is a collage of quotations about or paraphrases of references to Emily Dickinson's dog, Carlo, in *The Letters of Emily Dickinson*, vol. 2, eds. Thomas H. Johnson and Theodora Ward (Cambridge, MA, 1958), pp. 340, 358, 374, 404, 406, 408, 410, 415, 416, 423, 427, 431, 449, 450, 454, 461, 475.

"Composite": Roger Tory Peterson and Margaret McKenny, *A Field Guide to Wildflowers* (Boston, 1968), xxviii.

"Scottish Fleet Pattern Number Twenty-Four": Gladys Thompson, *Patterns for Guernseys, Jerseys and Arans* (New York, 1971), 112.

"They": Lorna Sage, *Moments of Truth* (New York, 2001), 129; Mary Wesley, *A Sensible Life* (New York, 1990), 168 (my paraphrase); Virginia Lee Burton, *Mike Mulligan and His Steam Shovel* (Boston, 1967), unpaged; Emily Dickinson, *The Letters of Emily Dickinson*, eds. Johnson and Ward (Cambridge, MA, 1958), p. 324; Jason Goodwin, *A Time for Tea* (New York, 1991), 159; Willa Cather, *Not Under Forty* (New York, 1936), v.

"Aragon": Stanza 4 quotes Mary Wesley, *Not That Sort of Girl* (London, 1987), 221.

"Subjects": Stanza 3, Jenny Uglow, *Nature's Engraver* (New York, 2006), 44, 117, 123, 241, 407; Stanza 5, Emily Dickinson, *The Poems of Emily Dickinson*, reading edition, ed. R. W. Franklin (Cambridge, 1999), #129; Stanza 6, Eric Siblin, *The Cello Suites* (New York, 2009), 38, 114.

"Singing in Yoghurt": Henry Hitchings, *The Secret Life of Words* (New York, 2008), 337.

ACKNOWLEDGMENTS

"He Was a Chartist": *The Massachusetts Review* 49/4 (Winter 2008: Grace Paley Issue)

"Stove Seasoning": *Barrelhouse* 7 (January 2009)

"Key": *New American Writing* 27 (Spring 2009)

"Flemish": *Boston Review* 34/2 (March/April 2009)

"Giant Culinary Otters": *Hanging Loose* 97 (Fall 2010)

"Wildwood Flower": *Hanging Loose* 95 (Fall 2009)

"You," "Joan of Arc High": *Fou* 3

"Harley Lyric": *notnostrums* 5

"His Mistress's Rights He Doth Defend": *Denver Quarterly* 43/4 (2009)

"Composite," "He Lives in Bayonne," "The Eaves": *Yew Journal* (July 2012)

"Scottish Fleet Pattern Number Twenty-Four": *A Public Space* 12 (Fall 2010)

"They": *New American Writing* 30 (May/June 2012)

"Marston": *Octopus* 13 (Spring 2010)

"Subjects" (excerpts): Stanza 1—Poets.org/The Academy of American Poets.
Stanzas 5 and 6—*Washington Square* 13 (Summer/Fall 2012)

"Singing in Yoghurt," "Kevin," "Year after Year": *Superstition Review* 5 (Spring 2010)

"At midnight the sound": *Hanging Loose* 95 (Fall 2009)

"Where": *Chiaroscuro* 6 (1985)

"The Scottish Play": *THEthe Poetry* (April 2012)

"Society": *LIT* 15/16 (Winter/Spring 2009)

"I'm going to Rupert's Land": *Electronic Poetry Review* (January 2008: Finale Issue)

"Scottish Fleet Pattern Number Twenty-Four" was made into a broadside
by Richard O'Russa for the Center for Book Arts, New York, 2012.